DESPERATE SEARCH

AS TOLD TO **BEN EAST**

ILLUSTRATED & DESIGNED BY JACK DAHL

EDITED BY JEROLYN NENTL AND DR. HOWARD SCHROEDER

Professor in Reading and Language Arts, Dept. of Elementary Education, Mankato State University

Library of Congress Cataloging in Publication Data.

East, Ben.
  Desperate search, as told to Ben East.
  (Survival)
  SUMMARY: While grouse hunting on a cool day in October, a 77-year-old man becomes lost in the woods of northern Michigan.
  (1. Survival. 2. Rescue work) I. Dahl, John I. II. Nentl, Jerolyn Ann. III. Schroeder, Howard. IV. Title. V. Series.
GV200.5.E27   614.8'77   79-5186
ISBN 0-89686-043-4 lib. bdg.
ISBN 0-89686-051-5 pbk.

International Standard Book Numbers:	Library of Congress
0-89686-043-4 Library Bound	Catalog Number:
0-89686-051-5 Paperback	79-5186

Adapted from the original publication *Narrow Escapes* by **Outdoor Life,** Copyright 1960.

CRESTWOOD HOUSE

**P.O. Box 3427
Hwy. 66 South
Mankato, MN 56001**

ABOUT THE AUTHOR...

Ben East has been an *Outdoor Life* staff editor since 1946. Born in southeastern Michigan in 1898, and a lifelong resident of that state, he sold his first story to *Outers Recreation* (later absorbed by *Outdoor Life*) in 1921. In 1926 he began a career as a professional writer, becoming outdoor editor of Booth Newspapers, a chain of dailies in eight major Michigan cities outside Detroit.

He left the newspaper job on January 1, 1946, to become Midwest field editor of Outdoor Life. In 1966 he was advanced to senior field editor, a post from which he retired at the end of 1970. Since then he has continued to write for the magazine as a contributing field editor.

Growing up as a farm boy, he began fishing and hunting as soon as he could handle a cane pole and a .22 rifle. He has devoted sixty years to outdoor sports, travel, adventure, wildlife photography, writing and lecturing. Ben has covered much of the back country of North America, from the eastern seaboard to the Aleutian Islands of Alaska, and from the Canadian arctic to the southern United States. He has written more than one thousand magazine articles and eight books. Today his by-line is one of the best known of any outdoor writer in the country. His outstanding achievement in wildlife photography was the making of the first color film ever taken of the Alaskan sea otter, in the summer of 1941.

In recent years much of his writing has dealt with major conservation problems confronting the nation. He has produced hard-hitting and effective articles on such environmentally destructive practices as strip mining, channelization, unethical use of aircraft to take trophy game, political interference in wildlife affairs, the indiscriminate use of pesticides and the damming of wild and scenic rivers and streams.

In 1973, he was signally honored when the Michigan Senate and House of Representatives adopted a concurrent resolution, the legislature's highest tribute, recognizing him for his distinguished contribution to the conservation of natural resources.

A FOREWORD TO DESPERATE SEARCH

In the fall of 1953 many Michigan newspapers carried a gripping story of a seventy-seven year old lost man. He was wandering in freezing weather in the wild and roadless woods in the Upper Peninsula of the state. He had no food, the story said, and no matches with which to start a fire.

A day or two later a second story reported that he had been found alive after three days and four nights of cold and hunger. A search team of twenty-five men had brought him safely out of the woods. His survival was all the more remarkable because of his age.

Those stories held special interest for me. For several years I had made it my business to track down men to whom such things had happened and get the complete story from them. Later I would put it in shape for use in Outdoor Life, the magazine for which I worked.

I phoned this elderly outdoorsman, whose name was Ed Downs, and then visited him at his home. He told me all that had happened during those terrible days and nights. Ed told of being cold, wet, hungry and exhausted, of hardly hoping to get out of the woods alive.

I explained that one reason Outdoor Life wanted his story was because of the way he had kept his head and refused to give up.

Finally I suggested that he must have some valuable advice to offer any person who gets lost in wild country. He agreed.

Mr. Downs' safety rules, as he related them to me, are set down at the end of this story. They are worth remembering. The rules are simple, but can save a life.

BEN EAST

It was Sunday, and Ed Downs wanted to spend a few hours grouse hunting. The weather was cool and cloudy, like it sometimes is on an October morning in the far north country. Downs looked at the sky and decided to take a chance. It looked as if it would turn out to be a nice warm day. He set out for the woods just behind his cabin. His wife was fixing an early Sunday dinner, so he promised to be home by noon.

Downs was an elderly man and he loved the woods. He had hunted and fished almost all of his seventy-seven years. A few years before, Downs and his wife had bought a cabin. It was in the Whitefish River Valley, of northern Michigan, just south of Lake Superior. The Downs' lived in Hastings, to the southwest, but spent much time at their cabin.

The Whitefish River country covered many acres of forest mixed with swamps and ridges of alder and cedar trees. There were some clearings here and there and a few old logging roads. That was all. Downs knew the country well. He had hunted deer in the northern part of the state for more than forty years. His first hunting trip had been with his father when he was only eight years old. From the beginning, he had liked the sport. Since then, Downs had hunted birds and deer, and had fished very often. He prided himself on his skills as a woodsman.

Downs was walking west as he set out from the cabin. To the north of his place was farmland belonging to a neighbor. To the south, was an old clearing where he had hunted many times in the past. Only woods, swamps, and streams flooded by beaver dams lay to the west. Downs took with him his twelve-gauge shotgun, his pipe and tobacco, and a pocketful of matches. It was to be a relaxing morning. He liked being in the woods even when he was not hunting.

Downs tramped through the woods for several hours without seeing a single grouse. Up one ridge and down another he went, but saw nothing. It was a good day for hunting. When he finally looked at his watch, it was close to one o'clock. Downs was going to be late for dinner.

9

Hurrying, Downs started back toward the cabin. He did not want to spoil his wife's Sunday dinner by being late. He walked steadily through the heavy timber, pushing his way through the dense brush. It was several hours before he felt something was wrong. He should have reached the cabin by this time. Instead, it was nowhere in sight. The thought that he might be lost never crossed his mind. Downs was sure that if he kept walking in one direction, he would make it home before dark.

The woods west of Downs' cabin was very thick. It would be easy for a beginner to get lost there. It would be even easier to get lost on a day such as this which was cloudy and calm. Without the sun and wind, it was hard to tell one direction from another. However, Downs gave no thought to such things. He was sure he was walking in the right direction. After all, the man was a skilled woodsman and knew the country well. Only one thing bothered him. He was very thirsty since he had hunted all day in dry country. There had been no water fit to drink, and Downs had not brought any along from home.

By now it was late afternoon. Downs heard a distant shot, off to what he believed was the north. Turning toward it, he walked for half an hour but found no one. Then he heard a second shot from

the opposite direction. He turned and again hurried toward it. He also fired a shot of his own, but there was no answer. Downs hurried, but found no one this time either. Had someone been looking for him? He was becoming confused. No longer was he sure of his directions. Following the shots had done nothing but confuse his sense of direction.

It was close to dark and Downs knew he would have to spend the night in the woods. He had not wanted to admit that he was lost. However, he had no other choice. He tried to think what he could do to help himself. Downs had only two matches left. The others had been used to light and relight his pipe that day. He still had most of his shotgun shells; one had been fired in answer to the hunter. He did not have his compass. It was in his hunting jacket hanging on a peg back in the cabin. He had not worn it because he thought it would be a warm day.

The first thing Downs did was fire two signal shots, in case somebody was looking for him. There was no reply, so he began to collect dry firewood. He had started too late, however. Daylight was fading. Since it was getting dark, Downs often tripped over logs and underbrush.

Darkness was settling over the woods, and with it came the chill of night. Downs was wearing only cotton clothing and light underwear. On his feet he wore a pair of old patched, rubber-bottomed boots. They were not enough to keep out the cold. He could find nothing with which to kindle a fire — no birch bark, pine twigs fat with pitch, nothing at all! He had no knife with him, so could not whittle any shavings.

Downs was not prepared for a night in the woods, but luck was with him. While looking for kindling, he found a big pine stump with its roots above ground. There was a small hollow between some of the roots that formed a cave. He could use it for shelter that night.

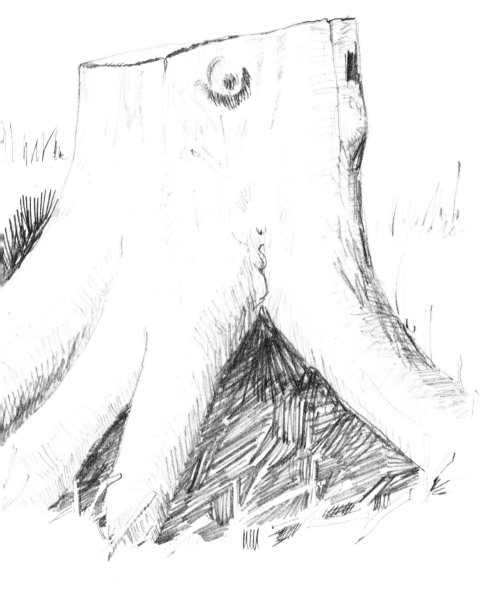

By now it was dark. More than ever, Downs wanted a fire to ward off the cold. He broke off a handful of small twigs from a dead tree, piled them beside the stump and struck a match. The wind caught the flame and blew it out. Quickly he struck a second match. Downs was worried now. It was the last match he had! A yellow flame sprang up from the twigs and he relaxed a bit. The twigs smoldered and a wisp of blue smoke rose toward his face. Then the flame of the match died. The twigs burned for a minute or two longer but never really caught fire. Finally, the fire went out.

All of a sudden, the woods seemed darker and more silent than ever before. He would have no fire to warm himself or keep him company during the night. Panic rose in his heart, and he began to fire several signal shots, one right after another. He did not stop until there were only three shells left. Two of the shells had been at the bottom of his jacket pocket for years. Now he found they would not even fit the chamber of his gun. That meant he had only one shell left that could be used. He decided to keep it. The signal shots had done no good at all. All Downs had succeeded in doing was waste his shells. The search for him had not begun.

Downs tried to make himself as comfortable for the night as he could. He made no bed, but scooped out some leaves and trash from the little hollow space beneath the stump. He broke off some big pieces of bark, and covered his legs with them.

That night he did not sleep well. He kept waking up, feeling very stiff and sore. Downs would move his arms and legs to work the chill out of them, then drift off to sleep again. Toward morning it started to rain, but it was a light rain and did not last long. The shelter of the stump kept his head and shoulders dry.

Downs' wife slept poorly that night, too. She had not been worried when he was late getting home for Sunday dinner. He had often come home an hour or two late from hunting trips. However, when he did not return by dark, she knew something was wrong. Had he suffered a heart attack or been hurt? Was he lost or ill? By then Mrs. Downs was truly worried. She called the Michigan State Police and asked for help. It did not take long for officers from Marquette to reach the cabin. They told her not to worry. But there was little they could do to find Downs that night. They drove along the main road until midnight, flashing a spotlight into the sky. The police had hoped Downs might see the light and signal back. Since there was no answer, the police knew a full-scale search was needed. The officers promised Mrs. Downs it would start in the morning. Then they went back to their post to organize a search and rescue team.

At daylight, the police were back. With them this time were sheriff's deputies and state officials. A large group of volunteers came to help look for Downs, too. A state police airplane was sent to fly low over the woods where they thought Downs was wandering.

The team searched all day but found nothing. Those walking the woods found no clues at all, and neither did those who were in the plane. Some began to believe that Ed Downs would not be found alive. They knew he was wearing only light clothing and did not have a compass. That was all they knew for sure.

Did he have a fire for warmth?

Had he found water?

Was he sick or hurt?

When the person lost in the woods is seventy-seven years old, a search team spares no effort. The searchers asked for a trained bloodhound, one of the oldest ways of tracking lost people. The closest dog of this type was owned by the State of Wisconsin, 150 miles away. The search team sent for it, but it arrived after dark. By that time, the ground was covered with a thick layer of frost. The dog was not able to pick up the track of

Ed Downs so the search was given up until daylight. The day had been a rough one for the searchers.

It had been a rough day for Downs, too. He awoke Monday at the first light of dawn, tired, stiff, and sore. The sky was still cloudy. Without the sun, he could not know for sure which direction he was walking. He rubbed the stiffness out of his legs and slowly got to his feet. His cabin was to the east, so he set out in the direction he thought was east. Downs was still sure that he would come to an old logging road leading back to the cabin within an hour or so.

Slowly he walked among the trees all morning. A little before noon, he came to the first water he had seen since leaving the cabin. It was a shallow pool among some dead leaves. The water was muddy and stale, but he was too thirsty to care. He lay on his stomach and drank. The water was cool on his lips, and it tasted good.

Downs drank as much as he could and then started walking again. An hour later he found a beaver pond on a small creek. He knew that he must have water to survive. Never again did he wander far from a stream. Downs was careful, however, not to fall into the water. Getting wet

could mean trouble. A man of his age, wearing such light clothing, could catch cold very easily in cool fall weather. Downs also stayed away from the big cedar swamps. He knew that it was not easy to go through such wet land.

It was Monday afternoon when Downs saw a squirrel. That was the first living thing which had crossed his path since he had left the cabin. He did not shoot it. He was not hungry enough to eat raw squirrel meat, and there was no fire to cook it.

Downs continued to walk all that day. He still felt he would find his own way out of the woods. Every so often he stopped for a short rest. Then force himself to his feet and walk onward. Morning faded into afternoon. Several times he tripped over brush and logs, even though it was still full daylight. Then darkness began settling over the woods again. Finally, at dusk, Downs gave up. He knew he would have to spend a second night in the woods.

In the fading light, Downs began to fix himself a place to sleep. He slept in the open this time, without the shelter of a stump which he had enjoyed the night before. He broke off evergreen branches for a bed and had enough left over to partly cover himself. That night the temperature fell to twenty-three degrees, nine degrees below freezing. Frost made the ground look like a blanket of silver.

Downs was miserable that night. The hours dragged by slowly as he lay shivering between the tree branches. His feet hurt from the cold. He knew he could warm them by walking or by jumping up and down, but Downs was too tired to get up. His wife would be very worried about him, he knew, but there was nothing that could be done about it.

Downs did not sleep much that night. He was anxious for morning to come so he could get back to the cabin. The old man did not fear for himself at all.

Downs was still sure he could find his own way out of the woods. He had heard planes several times on Monday, but did not know they were looking for him. Even if they were, he was not going to rely on them to get home. He did not need to be rescued. If he could just keep walking in a straight line toward the east . . .

Tuesday was much the same as Monday. Downs was up again at daybreak. He was cold and tired. Downs was getting weaker, but his hunger did not really bother him. He walked all day Tuesday, just as he had done on Monday. He was falling more often now, scratching and bruising himself. Later that day, he started using his gun as a cane to keep himself more steady on his feet. Tuesday was also the day he started losing things.

Downs had no way to light his pipe, now that his matches were gone. He missed not being able to smoke his pipe. In its place, he took from his pouch a pinch of tobacco to chew. That helped calm him. Later, when he reached for the pouch a second time, it was gone. Instead of putting it back into his pocket he had dropped it somewhere. He never was able to find it.

Downs also lost his glasses, his cap and one of his gloves. Things just did not seem quite right all that afternoon. He wandered back and forth, forgetting to walk in a straight line. His pant legs and jacket sleeves were torn. His boots were falling apart. By the end of the day, his mind was very confused. That night he again slept under some evergreen branches trying to keep himself warm. In the dark, he thought he heard deer and other animals in the woods around him.

The search team had walked through the woods all that day looking for Downs. They had started the bloodhound at the door of Downs' cabin Tuesday morning. Then they led him in the same direction Downs had gone. The dog barked a few times, but the trail was too faint to follow. The track was now forty-eight hours old. As the frosts of two nights had melted, any scent that might have been there was now washed away.

That afternoon, their luck improved. The first clue was found. It was the crude bed of branches where Downs had slept Monday night. No sign of a fire was found. The campsite answered two of the searchers' big questions. Now they knew they were looking for a lost hunter, not the body of a man dead from a heart attack. They were not looking for

a man who could not walk because he was ill or injured. The searchers also knew that Downs had no fire to warm himself or for signaling.

In spite of finding the campsite, the searchers went home Tuesday night feeling grim. As each day passed, there was less hope of finding Downs alive. Still, the searchers wanted to return in the morning for a third day of searching the woods. They asked that a helicopter join in the search Wednesday, in a final try to find him alive. Even Downs' wife feared rescue would come too late if he were not found Wednesday. She and the searchers agreed. Three days and three nights without food or fire were more than a man of that age could take.

Downs proved them all wrong. He could take a lot more.

Wednesday morning the sun rose in a cloudless sky, and at last Downs knew for sure which way was east. He started off in that direction, limping on blistered feet. His tired old legs would hardly carry his weight. He had to force himself to keep moving. With the sun pointing the way, he felt even more sure of himself. An hour or two of steady walking would bring him out onto the old logging road. The trouble now was that walking had become too much for him. He tripped again and again. Finally, he broke off a dry branch to use as a second cane.

Downs sat down to rest more and more often Wednesday. Each rest was longer than the one before. His strength was almost gone. He walked very slowly that morning, going a few yards and then stopping to rest.

Around noon, Downs heard a plane. He had heard aircraft several times Tuesday and Wednesday. He knew searchers would be looking for him by now, but none of the planes had been close enough to do any good. This time was different. This time the plane was flying straight toward him! Downs was resting in thick undergrowth along a creek. He jumped to his feet and waved his arms as hard as he could. The plane flew overhead so close he could see the two men in it. They were looking down over the side, but did not see him. The plane went off into the distance.

Downs sank onto a log, very tired and sad. He was still sitting on the log when he heard the plane make a wide turn in the distance and head back toward him. It swept overhead again, a little farther away this time. Downs quickly put his one good shell into the chamber of his gun and fired, but the little gun was no match for the roar of the plane. The sound of the shot was drowned out by the hum of the engine. The pilot flew on, not knowing he had twice passed over the missing man. Two more

times, the plane passed within Downs' sight. Each time it was a little farther away.

About the same time Downs saw the search plane, ground searchers found the spot where he had spent Tuesday night. It told them that Downs was still alive and that he was still without fire. It did not tell them much else. If Downs was to be found now, it would be by men on foot. It would have to be by a rescue team searching the woods with more care than ever before. They would have to look behind every log and under every tree. Missing any clue at all could mean death for Downs, if he were not already dead. It was no longer a job for aircraft.

That afternoon, the pilots returned to their home bases. Plans were made to build the ground team up to three hundred persons Thursday morning. No one talked about it, but they all knew the truth. It takes more searchers to find a dead person than a live one.

When the airplane did not see him, Downs began to lose hope. He had not seen a landmark he recognized since Sunday morning. Somehow, he thought to himself, he must have missed the old logging road after all. He was getting very depressed. Giving up, he started to wander aimlessly. He decided it no longer mattered which way he went.

After awhile, he found a deer trail and followed it. At one point he came to a fallen log. As he painfully climbed over it, he broke off a small dead tree that was in his way. He wandered on some more, but soon he was back at the same fallen log. He knew it was the same one by the broken snag. That meant Downs was walking in circles. He knew he should not do that, but didn't know which way to go. It did not seem to matter. Later, he crossed the fallen log a third time. This time he was not even able to decide if he was going in the same direction or not. Was he backtracking on himself? It troubled the old man, but once more he didn't seem to care.

Downs had little sense of direction left now. He moved very slowly. He would take a few shaky steps, sink down to rest, and then stagger onward once more. An hour or so before sunset he started to prepare for the night. It would be his fourth night in the woods. Downs broke off a few evergreen branches for a bed. Too tired to do any more, he sat on a log by a beaver pond to rest. There he sat, bent over with his chin in his hands. Downs was almost unconscious.

Suddenly, he heard a noise in the brush nearby! He looked up and saw a man walking along, glancing first to his left and then to his right. The man had not yet seen him. Downs gathered what strength he had left and let out a loud yell.

"Hey, there!"

The shout was loud and clear, and the man walking on the ridge quickly turned around. He was about forty yards from the beaver pond where Downs sat. The man stared toward the pond.

What he saw startled him even more than the loud yell. Downs looked more like a live scarecrow than a man.

The searcher fired three shots signaling that Downs had been found. Then he started running toward the pond. Downs pulled himself up from the log and called in a tired voice:

"I'm all right. Take your time."

When the man got closer, Downs saw that it was one of his neighbors, a trapper named Bill who lived not far from his cabin. Bill hardly recognized Downs. The frail, older man could hardly stand. His gray cotton pants hung in rags and his jacket was tattered and torn. He was without gloves or a hat. His thin white hair framed a face sunken from hunger and full of scratches. The stubble of a gray beard made Downs look older than he was.

Bill's shots had been heard by other searchers, and help was soon there. They helped carry Downs out of his beloved woods. They took him to a Marquette hospital, and that night Downs rested between warm woolen blankets and drank hot soup. It was quite a change from the four long days and three cold nights in the forest.

Downs came through his ordeal in good condition, although he had lost sixteen pounds. He was black and blue, and had many scratches from falling so often. His worn out boots had rubbed his feet

raw. Still, Downs was lucky. No serious side effects arose to cause him further health problems. Within four days he was out of the hospital.

Downs was very surprised when he talked to the state police. They told him that at no time had he been more than four miles from his own cabin! If he had stayed by the stump where he spent Sunday night, he would have been rescued the next day.

Downs' big mistake was being too sure of himself. It came close to costing him his life. For those who go into the woods he has three rules:

1) Never go into the woods without a compass, a knife, and a good supply of matches. Take them with you even if you know the country well.

2) Keep your matches for an emergency. Don't waste them!

3) If you realize you are lost, or cannot get back to camp before dark, stop and build a fire. Stay in one place until help comes.

"Wandering won't get you anywhere," he advises. "It's no good to travel unless you are sure of your directions and know exactly where you are going. Don't count on your judgement to take the place of a compass. Don't be overly confident about getting out by yourself. Being lost is a terrible experience. Four days of it is for sure, long enough!"

Stay on the edge of your seat.

Read:

FROZEN TERROR

DANGER IN THE AIR

MISTAKEN JOURNEY

TRAPPED IN DEVIL'S HOLE

DESPERATE SEARCH

FORTY DAYS LOST

FOUND ALIVE

GRIZZLY!